Letters Never Sent

By
Ina Fisher

MAPLE
PUBLISHERS

Letters Never Sent

Author: Ina Fisher

Copyright © Ina Fisher (2025)

The right of Ina Fisher to be identified as author of this work has been asserted by the author in accordance with section 77 and 78 of the Copyright, Designs and Patents Act 1988.

First Published in 2025

ISBN 978-1-83538-819-8 (Paperback)
     978-1-83538-820-4 (Hardback)
     978-1-83538-821-1 (E-Book)

Book cover design and Book layout by:
    White Magic Studios
    www.whitemagicstudios.co.uk

Published by:
    Maple Publishers
    Fairbourne Drive, Atterbury,
    Milton Keynes,
    MK10 9RG, UK
    www.maplepublishers.com

A CIP catalogue record for this title is available from the British Library.

All rights reserved. No part of this book may be reproduced or translated by any form or by any means, electronic or mechanical, including photocopying, recording or by any information storage and retrieval system without written permission from the author.

The book is a work of fiction. Unless otherwise indicated, all the names, characters, places and incidents are either the product of the author's imagination or used in a fictitious manner. Any resemblance to actual people living or dead, events or locales is entirely coincidental, and the Publisher hereby disclaims any responsibility for them.

Contents

- Loving a Mirage 5
- Forbidden Comfort 6
- Conflicted Love 7
- Bruised Affection 8
- Heart's Deception 9
- Fading Fairytale 10
- Heart's Missing Key 11
- Love's Lingering Ghost 12
- Dancing in Uncertainty 13
- Falling Through Frayed Love 14
- Trapped in Time 15
- Teaspoons 16
- The Reread Script 17
- Hidden Lovers Dance 19
- The Lie of Time 20
- The Puppet's Lament 21
- Unspoken Passion 22
- Tapestry of You 23
- Words like Chains 24
- Words like Chains: His POV 25
- Your Puppet 26
- What Remains 27
- Darkness Consumes Me 29
- Laundry 30
- Crumbs I Deserve 31
- Crimson Heart 32
- The Edge of Empty 34
- Splintered Heart 35

- The Weight of Wounds 36
- The Weight of Giving 37
- In the Wake of Silence 38
- Before He Leaves Me 39
- What You Took 40
- Splintered Throne 41
- From Flame to Shadow 42
- Forever His 44
- Love Like Rain 45
- Chasing Quicksand 46
- Fragments of the Giver 48
- The Only Road I Know 49
- My Veins Run Dry 50
- The Glow That Fades 51
- Never Loved Out Loud 53
- When the Weather Texts Back 54
- Where Wounds Are 55
- Between Each Relapse 57
- The Name You Buried 58
- Too Sweet, Too Loud 60
- Ink This Pain 61
- Poison and Frost 63
- Letting Go In Pieces 65
- Holding Until it Hurts 67
- Small Enough to Stay 68
- Fitting Into Your Rain 69
- Learning to Live 70

Loving a Mirage

He won't change to who you want
You need to realise that,
He'll hurt you over and over
And he won't look back.
He says he likes your body
And I do think that is true,
But what about what's deep within
The things he barely bothered to ask you?
He traces his hands over your body
He doesn't ask about your scars,
Because to him you're just a person
But to you it's written in the stars.
He didn't congratulate you on your job
Because he doesn't care,
You know every detail of his life
But he just cares what you wear.
So, he won't change to who you want
You can't make him someone he's not,
You keep telling yourself he cares for you
But really, he just thinks you're hot.

Forbidden Comfort

Always on your terms
Never mine,
But lying next to you
Was my favourite crime.

Letters Never Sent

Conflicted Love

You tell me what I want to hear
It makes me stay,
I can never say no to you
Though I wish I could, every day.
Tangled together
Your heart and mine,
But you're also intertwined with her
While my heart is on the line.
Do you care or do you not
I'm not sure I'll ever know,
You sweettalk me so that I stay
Emotions overflow.
You complain about her, say I'm yours
If only she knew,
I should tell her everything
But instead, I cling on to you.
I just want you to want me
In all the ways I do,
Two souls intertwined
If only you knew.

Bruised Affection

I tried to do the healing,
My heart just keeps on bleeding.
Splintered, bruised, purple and blue,
I really wanted it to be you.

Heart's Deception

It's funny how we remember things
Things that aren't quite true,
King, loving, respectful
That's how I remember you.
But there runs my stupid mind
Playing tricks on me,
Turns out you were none of these things
But I guess you see what you want to see.
We have excuses in common
We both make them for you,
But I caught a glimpse of your true colours
The you I never knew.
I loved everything about you
But you weren't really real,
You gave me back my heart in a million pieces
How am I supposed to feel?

Fading Fairytale

Rose tinted glasses
Glued to my eyes,
My vision is clouded
Until the fairytale dies.
The glasses started to crack
They let me see the bad,
I tried to ignore it
You continued to make me sad.
The good became bad
The rose became blue,
I tried my hardest to cling on
I could never say no to you.
It's not me, it's you
We both need time to heal,
Desperate to break the cycle
Of all this pain I feel.
Always on your terms
Your mood determines mine,
You tell me it was real
Right person, wrong time.

Letters Never Sent

Heart's Missing Key

My concept of my worth forever shifted
I gave you all of me,
I just wanted one piece of me back
But I don't have the key.
I gave my everything, my entire heart
And you kept it in a box,
Occasionally opening it and pulling my strings
I wish I could turn back the clocks.
Pins and needles in my soul
I feel you when I'm sad,
I associate that feeing with you
I wish you just made me mad.
But I am a forgiver
I'll make excuses so it's not your fault,
I'm sure it wasn't intentional
To lace my open wounds with salt.

Love's Lingering Ghost

September's not the same now
Not since I met you,
Everywhere is a reminder
Of all the things we used to do.
I've never craved someone's attention
Not like I did from him,
I just can't let you go
You tore me limb from limb.
I don't think I'll ever get over it
I've never loved that deep,
I search for you in everyone
Only finding you in sleep.
You gave love a whole different meaning
I've never felt like that before,
The pain I feel just gets worse
Heart bleeding, soul sore.
But you won't let go of me either
You check in all the time,
Tell me you miss us too
Is wanting you back a crime?
If it is, I'll take the punishment
Lock me in a cell,
It can't be worse than where I am now
You've already sentenced me to hell.

Dancing in Uncertainty

In the shadows of doubt, I lost myself
My soul is torn, my heart is weak,
Caught in a dance of love and lust
He loves me not; he loves me deep.
He looks at me, with those eyes
His gaze a puzzle I cannot solve,
The pieces don't fit, it doesn't make sense
Does he love me or am I just involved?
I linger in the silence of his indecision
One day he loves me, the next we're friends,
Caught in a web of longing and division
I wait patiently but the cycle never ends.
He kisses my lips, he feels so safe
Like a bittersweet symphony,
Our bodies fit just right together
Leaving me lost in a sea of uncertainty.
I yearn for clarity; he leaves me hanging
I hold on tight, afraid to let go,
In his silence I find my pain
But in his arms my heart feels whole.

Ina Fisher

Falling Through Frayed Love

The safety net of our love
Woven with threads of doubt,
Holes gaping wide
Where trust is worn out.
I leap into the unknown
Hoping you'll catch me and prove you care,
But uncertainty lingers
A heavy burden to bear.
I slip through the holes
Reach out for your hand,
I can't cling on to the net
But I keep trying, hoping you'll catch me before I land.
Your fingers slip through mine
As they used to through my hair,
I fall into the darkness
All that's left to do is despair.
The safety net that once was
Is now riddled with holes and thread,
Just like my heart in your hands
I'm left in a sea of red.

Trapped in Time

Nobody could love you more than me
The words pierce my soul,
Because if love is the cruel game you play
How can I ever feel whole?
Love is supposed to be warm
But our love turned cold,
Love is supposed to be safe
But you made me promise no one could be told.
Alone in my feelings
You call me again,
Ask me what I've been up to
If I'm seeing other men.
But I'm still in that time loop
Every day is the same,
No way back or forward
I just want you to love me again.

Ina Fisher

Teaspoons

It felt like love when you whispered my name,
But your sweet words were all part of your game.
You say that you love me, you want me to stay,
But your promises fade as night turns to day.
"Get home safe" you tell me, concern in your voice,
But love is just a pretence, and lust is your choice.
My heart clings to the sugar you feed me each night,
Teaspoons of sweetness to keep hope alight.
I'm lost in the passion, unable to leave,
Desiring the dream, desperate to believe.
Yet deep down, I know, in the light of day,
Your love fades to shadows, and I'm led astray.
But here I remain, in love's cruel embrace,
Hoping one day you'll cherish my face.
Though trapped in the cycle of yearning and doubt,
I dream of love where truth will break out.
Until then, I hold on, my heart in disguise,
Living off teaspoons, and your sweet, bitter lies.

Letters Never Sent

The Reread Script

He whispers, "this is the last time"
His words a familiar refrain,
A promise woven with moonlight
But destined to end in pain.
His touch ignites my longing
A flame that consumes my heart,
In the shadowed dance of moonlight
Where me meet and then depart.
His love a fleeting phantom
Vanishing with the dawn,
Leaving me in silken sheets
To wonder where he's gone.
I fall for his sweet deception
In a cycle without end,
For the heart believes in fairytales
Even when they are pretend.
Once more, he says it's over
This time will be the end,
But I know the script by heart now
And the pain that it will send.
His love a cruel illusion
A lie that feels so true,
Leaves me in endless yearning
For the dream I thought I knew.

Ina Fisher

I drift in endless twilight
Between hope and despair,
Knowing this endless cycle
Will keep me trapped in his snare.

Hidden Lovers Dance

In shadows cast by secret nights,
A love so twisted, hidden from light.
With tender words and fingers traced,
A stolen world, a hidden place.
In hushed embraces, whispers low,
Uncontrollable longing starts to grow.
In fleeting moments, hearts entwine,
A passion deep, a love divine.
Behind closed doors, away from sight,
We find our refuge in the night.
A dance of souls, so pure and free,
In secret shadows just you and me.
Yet morning breaks, our words must fade,
As light reveals the roles we've played.
But in the dark, we'll find our way,
Back together, where mistakes replay.

Ina Fisher

The Lie of Time

Time should heal but it doesn't
The weeks just pass me by,
Memories poison in my body
Was everything a lie?
It kills me slowly like a cancer in my soul
And you don't even notice,
You watched the life drain from my eyes
Brought my pain back into focus.
I'm getting tired of being strong
Can you give me a second if you have time?
I feel your fingers trace circles in my palm
I need to know these feelings weren't just mine.
For though they say I'll heal with time
And find a love that's fresh and new,
My heart is bound with every line,
Of a story that began with you.

Letters Never Sent

The Puppet's Lament

You, my constant, the cause and cure of endless pain
I love you, you casually confessed,
So, in the mirror, I morph to fit your mould
My clothes fall to the ground as you get me undressed.
Your words slice through me
Your blade cold and sharp,
In the darkness of lost love
Rainy memories, and my broken heart.
I change for you, reshape my soul
A puppet to your whims and desires,
You pull my strings and let them go again
Lies whispered, my heart acquires.
Your indifference stings like a thousand cuts
Piercing my soul, I question why,
I tune out the pain, but it consumes my heart
Yet for your love, I'd bleed myself dry.
Bound to you I lose my faith
I lay there limp, you pull my strings,
In your embrace, both cold and warm
A collection of hurt, where brokenness clings.

Ina Fisher

Unspoken Passion

In silent rooms where whispers die,
Out secret love must pass us by.
A tangled web of hidden ties,
In stolen moments, truth belies.
In daylights glare, our glances stay,
Forbidden touch, kept far at bay.
A hidden fire, a veiled embrace,
In public eyes we leave no trace.
Our lips abound by silent thread,
In quiet corners, words unsaid.
A twisted bond, a secret pact,
In this affair we can't retract.
The world outside is none the wise,
To this secret love that truth denies.
In private worlds our hearts entwine,
Yet never speak of what is mine.
A coded language in our eyes,
The truth beneath our practiced lies.
In hushed retreats we dare to feel,
A love that's twisted, yet so real.
When morning breaks, the silence grows,
Our love a river no one knows.
In this twisted fate, we're bound to hide,
A silent passion we can't confide.

Tapestry of You

You don't cross my mind, you live in its core
A constant presence I cannot shake,
Every breath and thought you consume
Interlinked so deep it makes me ache.
Like whispers of dawn, in shadows you hide
You dwell in the corners, the light and the dark,
With every heartbeat, your essence remains
In dreams and in waking, you leave your mark.
In the tapestry of time, your thread is spun
No fleeting moment, no passing glance,
Through all life's changes, you are my constant
Keeping me trapped in this trance.

Ina Fisher

Words like Chains

His words cut deep, like shards of glass,
Etched into my skin, scars that last.
In his eyes I'm tiny and small,
A whisper of worth, eclipsed by his call.
He calls me names that burn and stain,
Choosing his words just to cause pain.
In every syllable, a cage I find,
A prison built in the corners of my mind.
I once was whole, knew my own name,
Now I'm lost beneath his taunts and shame.
In mirrors, a stranger meets my gaze,
A reflection blurred by his cruel ways.
I question every step I take,
Afraid of each choice I make.
Is there a way to set me free,
From the chains of his cruelty?
In the darkness of his words, I drown,
He reigns over me, wearing the crown.
His cruelty a storm that never ends,
Sealing my fate, never to transcend.

Words like Chains: His POV

I wield my words with calculated aim,
To make her feel small, to reinforce my claim.
I see her shrinking, cowering in my clasp,
Her worth dissolving as a tighten my grasp.
I call her names that sear and brand,
Words meant to break her, crafted by my hand.
Each insult is a chain I design,
To bind her spirit and make it mine.
Once she was whole, standing strong and sure,
But I've broken her down, made her insecure.
In mirrors, she sees the scars I've sown,
A reflection blurred by the seeds I've grown.
I watch her hesitate with every choice,
Silencing her once confident voice.
The control consumes me, it makes me feel strong,
For in her submission, I feel I belong.
I know the power I wield is cruel,
But it fills the void, so over her I rule.

Ina Fisher

Your Puppet

You treated me like your puppet
I would do anything you say,
I'd drop everything and run to you
No matter the time, place, or day.
You had me on a lead
I was under your spell,
Completely consumed by your so called 'love'
But you dragged me through hell.
I don't know why it took me so long to see
You were bad for my heart,
And you stole so much love from me
While you tore me apart.
Searching for the missing pieces of me
I can't seem to retrieve,
I want the person I was before you back
When I wore my heart on your sleeve.

What Remains

His favourite colour was red, so I bled myself dry,
Gave him all that I had beneath a merciless sky,
I laid down my heart like a sacrificial flame,
And tore myself open again and again.
With every touch, my world unravelled in shame,
Yet I whispered in darkness, calling his name.
He tore through my soul, leaving nothing but scars,
Taking all that I was beneath the moon and the stars.
In his eyes, I sought the comfort of light,
Yet found only shadows that deepened the night.
Still, he returned, insatiable and blind,
While I offered my heart, my body, my mind.
I craved his affection, his slightest embrace,
But he ripped out my heart, leaving an unfillable space.
Shattered and hollow, collapsed on the floor,
Alone and exposed, he left me once more.
Yet even as shadows encircled my heart,
I gave all I had while he tore me apart.
In the silence between us, where promises break,
I yearned for a love he would never forsake.
For the taste of his love, I surrendered myself,
Though he left me broken, crying for help.
In the shadow of longing, where lost lovers cry,

I bleed myself dry beneath an indifferent sky.
Through the pain and the tears, I held on tight,
To the echoes of him that filled the night.
Now I lie in the ruins, in the grave of my shame,
Surrendering once more, now only whispers remain.

Darkness Consumes Me

I don't want to do this anymore
I've lost the fight within,
Believed that I was crazy
You are my biggest sin.
You couldn't love me truly
Not in the way I needed,
Now I'm just a shadow here
Where I once felt so completed.
The black hills didn't scare me
But the darkness grew inside,
I don't know what to do
There's nowhere left to hide.
It all tastes like poison now
With every breath I take,
Your kisses full of cyanide
Feed my heart that aches.
Left behind in love's cruel wake
As he drifts into the night,
I'll be the once to stay
As I'm consumed by quiet plight.

Ina Fisher

Laundry

I think about you whilst I do laundry
Folding the memories I can't forget,
The way you looked when you were sleeping
Breathing heavy, eyes half-set.
I make breakfast and I think about
How you'd eat without a word,
You never took me out to dinner
But in my mind the past is blurred.
I focus on fleeting moments
The brush of hands, the stolen glance,
I replay them like a fairytale
Blind to the broken romance.
You rarely spoke with warmth or meaning
But in my mind, you always did,
I paint the nights you left me lonely
Crafting tales that never lived.
I treasure silence, fill the gaps
With words you never said,
It's easier to hold the scraps
Then admit the love was dead.
So, I fold the truth and put it down
Soft echoes of a faded rhyme,
I slip back into the sheets you once graced
Dreaming of illusions of lost time.

Crumbs I Deserve

I take the crumbs you leave behind
Scattered pieces, small and spare,
A glance, a word, a fleeting smile
I hold them close, hoping they're really there.
I take off my glasses, let things blur
So, I won't see how little's there,
The edges soften, truths distort
And in the haze, I pretend you care.
I settle for scraps, like a rabid dog
When what I need is so much more,
But I've trained myself to feel content
With the crumbs scattered on the floor.
I close my eyes and tell myself
This must be love, this must be right,
But I can't see clearly, I don't want to know
How dim it is without your light.
I should reach for more, demand what is fair
But I'd rather settle for what you give,
So, I take the crumbs and swallow them down
Convincing myself this is how I want to live.

Ina Fisher

Crimson Heart

My heart spills crimson on the floor
A river of loss, a bloodied stain,
Each beat a whisper of what was
A haunting echo of your name.
The memories cut like jagged glass
Each shard a promise, sharp and clear,
I trace the edges, feel the pain
A deep red ribbon of my fear.
You were the light that filled my days
Now darkness is all I can find,
I search for comfort in the void
But find only shadows, cold and unkind.
I see your smile in every dream
A ghost that dances just out of reach,
The laughter fades, replaced by cries
A lesson love was meant to teach.
The nights bleed into endless hours
Where silence drips like drops of rain,
I drown in thoughts of what we lost
In this unrelenting, aching pain.
Each memory pulses, raw and red
A bitter reminder of love's cruel fight,
You were my sun, now just a ghost

A flame extinguished, snuffed from light.
I wear my heartbreak like a scar
An emblem of a love betrayed,
And as a bleed in quiet despair
I wonder why my heart was made.
To love so fiercely, only to break
To taste the sweetness turned to sour,
In the ruins of us, I stand alone
A crimson shadow of love that ran out of power.

Ina Fisher

The Edge of Empty

The world is draped in muted grey
A silence I can't break,
No need for words, I fall apart
It's only for you I ache.
I long to hear the quiet sound
Your blinking soft and slow,
The rhythm of your heartbeat near
The steadiness I know.
We were so intertwined it seemed
Like threads that gently weave,
With you the world felt soft and clear
Now I just want to leave.
I'd drive for miles just to have
Five minutes by your side,
A friend or more, the question remains
But to you my soul is tied.
Each moment felt so easy once
Now I'm lost, undone,
Without you here the road is dark
And I don't like who I've become.
You're slipping further every day
The light is gone and I'm afraid,
Without you everything feels wrong
A bond begins to fade.

Splintered Heart

In the depths of my heart, I feel a weight,
The burden of love that has sealed my fate.
Maybe I'm destined to love all so deep,
With no one returning he love that I reap.
A shattered heart, like broken glass it lies,
Each piece reflecting the tears in my eyes.
I give so much love, yet feel it's in vain,
Wondering if I've earned this deep aching pain.
Did I do something wrong in a past life,
Is love just meant for some, while it cuts me like a knife?
No romantic embrace, just longing and ache,
As I pour my heart out, in hopes it won't break.

Ina Fisher

The Weight of Wounds

Again and again, you let me down,
I crave your love, but I look like a clown.
Your fleeting touch warms me for days,
But I can't find my way, I'm trapped in your maze.
You've reshaped my soul, I've lost my way,
Whenever you leave, I beg you to stay.
Once pink cheeked and whole, now I'm a ghost,
Chasing reflections of who I miss most.
I carved his name into my heart,
As he promised me we'd never part.
But he let me down again and again,
Until it drove me completely insane.
My hands held on to fraying threads,
Words unspoken, left unsaid.
I hope life is kind and gentle to you,
Though I know you don't wish the same for me too.
Loneliness fills me like bitter wine,
I sip it slowly, line by line.
Maybe one day I'll learn the word no,
But until then I hope from this pain I can grow.

The Weight of Giving

I've given all I am
Like oceans drained to their last drop,
Each thread of love pulled out and stitched into others
I saved none for me, I don't know how to stop.
My heart beats slow, it's fraying fast
Its edges worn and raw,
In every thread I once held tight
Now bleeds from every flaw.
In darkness comes death's cold kiss
Its knife pressed so deep,
While bones that bore the weight of light
Now tremble, break and weep.
My soul's a patchwork, falling apart
Each thread begins to fall,
For I've given all the love I had
There's nothing left at all.

Ina Fisher

In the Wake of Silence

I built my hope on borrowed light,
That shone through the cracks of night.
Whispers clung to breathless air,
Promises made of empty prayer.
Each passing hour stretched like years,
Time eroded faith to fears.
I carved his name in fragile stone,
He bled me dry, leaving me alone.
My hangs clung onto fading thread,
When I had nothing left, he left me for dead.
Loneliness consumed me like poisoned wine,
I sipped it slowly, line by line.
But the dawn broke, with no sign,
No shadow fell to meet with mine.
And in that silence, raw and stark,
I learned the language of the dark.
There is no saviour, no guiding flame,
Just echoes known for causing pain.
The ache of being left behind,
Only you can heal my restless mind.
And so, I stand, unrescued still,
A ghost in search of its own will.
The world moved on, the night turned grey,
And I stood still as the world slipped away.

Before He Leaves Me

I've given my body more times than I know,
Thinking each time it might make him show.
Some piece of his heart that he's hiding away,
A love that would linger, a reason to stay.
Yet here I am waiting, holding my breath,
Curled up in silence, feeling like death.
His phone lights up, and he's lost in its glow,
My heart skips a beat, but he doesn't know.
I tell myself stories over and over,
Trying to breathe, just to keep my composure.
But every missed text, every call left unseen,
Feels like the end of all that I've been.
My heart beats fast, it races and falls,
My anxious mind building towering walls.
Guarding the fear that he'll vanish in time,
Like everyone else, without reason or rhyme.
I know it's not healthy, the weight that I hold,
The hope wrapped in terror; the warmth turned to cold.
But here in this pain, I've buried my trust,
Too afraid to let go yet crumbling to dust.
So, I sit here in pieces, waiting to see,
Just how long it will be before he leaves me.

Ina Fisher

What You Took

You'll probably think this poem's about you,
A truth wrapped in silence I said I outgrew.
But here it lies, a wreck on the floor,
A heart turned to pieces, shattered once more.
"Why her?", I ask, when I gave you my all,
I stood in your silence, took every fall.
I offered you pieces of me, raw, untamed,
But you built your walls and left me unnamed.
All of my hours, my hopes, and my grace,
Were wasted like I was some hollow space.
I gave you my future, my here and my now,
But it slipped through your fingers, not telling me how.
Stitching together the lies that you told,
While I was left in pieces out in the cold.
You took what was mine and left me to drown,
In the shadows I crawl, while you wear your crown.

Letters Never Sent

Splintered Throne

Maybe I need you, maybe that's my curse,
To reach for warmth just for it to disperse.
To feel the ache of your touch for days,
While you drift away, my heart decays.
I love you in spite of the hollow ache,
The words unsaid while I lie awake.
I cling to moments that shimmer and flee,
Where you're almost mine, where you almost see.
But more often than not you're a shadow there,
A phantom smile, a vacant stare.
Your voice so soft can cut like knives,
Your eyes so warm tell a thousand lies.
And I, the fool with hope that won't tire,
Stay close to the flame that becomes my fire.
It warms, it sears, it leaves me burned,
But I need it to breathe, lessons unlearned.
So maybe I need you, maybe it's true,
Even when loving you tears me in two.
But the tears are real, and the nights are long,
And leaving my heart with you sometimes feels wrong.
I wish you could know the weight of this love,
The burden I carry, the push and the shove.
Yet here I remain on this splintered throne,
Why does loving you make me feel so alone?

Ina Fisher

From Flame to Shadow

I once was a flame, fierce and untamed,
Burning with purpose, unbroken, unclaimed.
I filled every room with my presence so free,
A warmth in my heart that could spread through the sea.
But then you came close, and I let you inside,
A flicker of trust, I sought to abide.
You vowed to stay always, and I gave you my trust,
Now all that remains is a shadow of dust.
Why do I reach for you just to feel whole?
Why does your absence now shatter my soul?
You take me for granted, I'm lost in your game,
You've broken me open, and I've lost my name.
Once radiant and bold, I could light up the skies,
But now I'm a shadow, lost in your lies.
The sun in me flickers, it splutters and dies,
A fading reflection, in lost, empty skies.
The light was once blinding, now barely a spark,
You left me to wither, to drown in the dark.
I hate how you've changed me, how small I've become,
I used to be fire, now I'm a whisper, undone.
Where once there was warmth, now cold winds prevail,

The sky full of colour has now turned so pale.
No stars left to guide me, no moon up above,
Just endless blackness, devoid of all love.
I was once the sun, a fire in the sky,
But now I am nothing, with no soul left to try.

Ina Fisher

Forever His

He saves me for last, like he knows I'll wait,
Patience in silence, where love meets fate.
I'd let him talk forever, his voice a hymn,
While my eyes drink deep, watching him.
He takes my time like it's his to keep,
A thief in the night, stealing sleep.
I love him like he ticking loves the clock,
My time's running out, but I won't ever stop.
His name lingers sweet on my eager tongue,
But I ache for the words he's left unsung.
He calls when he wants, a siren's tone,
And I answer, though I know I'm alone.
His breath is fire against my skin,
A fleeting moment I long to begin.
I want to be more than a passing flame,
To hold his heart, to share his name.
But he's the storm I can't outrun,
The moon I chase though he hides in the sun.
If love's a crime, I'll take the blame,
For I've been burning just hearing his name.
I hold him tighter, no words can convey,
That I'd give him my life if he asked me to stay.

Love Like Rain

I love him like the rain loves the storm,
And though it chills me, I'll keep myself warm.
I know it hurts, but I'll never let go,
Like I river that keeps flowing, though the current's too slow.
He comes and he goes, like clouds in flight,
Filling my world, then fading from sight.
I wait for his chaos, his beautiful pain,
Like parched earth aching for rain.
His touch a thunder, his voice a roar,
A sweetness I crave like a tale from ancient lore.
Each lightening flash is a promise, a plea,
That he might hold what can set me free.
I'll love him still through the cold and the strife,
Like the storm loves the sky it tears with its knife.
Though I break in his wake, I'll come back for more,
For love like his is worth the war.

Ina Fisher

Chasing Quicksand

It started with the sound of leaving,
A slam, a silence, a heart still grieving.
You were my first absence, a hollowed-out man,
Gone before I could understand.
Now I find pieces of you in everyone I crave,
Chasing their shadows, becoming their slave.
They're drawn to my fractures, my desperate ache,
I cling too tightly, and they always break.
Love, for me, is a frantic plea,
A lifeboat in a stormy sea.
I wrap myself around the fleeting and flawed,
Begging for permanence, I sit there in awe.
I carve myself smaller to make them stay,
Offer my soul on the ground I lay.
Yet each performance ends the same,
They vanish, leaving me clutching blame.
Do I seek them, or do they seek me?
This cruel pattern I can't seem to flee.
Their leaving confirms what I've always known,
I am unworthy of being someone's home.
But oh, the clawing, the desperate tether,
I promise forever, though they're gone whenever.
I break myself just to hold them tight,
Fighting for ghosts in a losing fight.

And here I stand, shards in my hands,
Dreaming of love but chasing quicksand.
This ruinous cycle, my heart in a cage,
A lifetime of wounds, a mounting rage.
In the depths of despair, I search for a spark,
But the flame flickers out, leaving only the dark.
So, I gather my pieces, though sharp and stained,
A heart full of longing, forever pained.

Ina Fisher

Fragments of the Giver

Always the saviour, never the saved,
I give all I am 'til my heart is frayed.
Always the artist, never the muse,
I deal with the pain like it's something I choose.
I try to love, but they say I'm too much,
A heart to heavy, a soul out of touch.
I hand out my love like my heart's an endless pit,
But I'm a puzzle so broken, never the right fit.
Everything I hold falls apart in a breath,
Shattered in seconds, undone by regret.
I thought I could soar, but I only fell,
A dreamer who crashes, under his spell.
Always the jinx, never the luck,
A whispered curse that won't come unstuck.
When will it end, this endless descent,
When will I find where my loneliness went.
I'm tired of loving and giving it my all,
Of standing so strong, just waiting to fall.

The Only Road I Know

I've stared at the finish line so long,
Afraid I've done it all wrong.
I turn and walk a thousand paces,
Yet end up back in the same places.
I always find my way to you,
No matter what I'm going through.
I try to leave, but I always stay,
In the echo of yesterday.
Back to you I always go,
Even when it hurts me so.
You push me down, then pull me near,
And I come back, nothing is clear.
I wonder if I'll miss the pain,
And if I'll ever break the chain.
But all I do is go back to you,
That's all I know how to do.

Ina Fisher

My Veins Run Dry

I bled for you, a river slow,
Each drop a piece of me you'll never know.
But you never looked, you never cared,
A quiet scream in the silence we shared.
I gave my heart, my soul, my skin,
But you never saw the storm within.
I was never the one, always the ghost,
The one before the one you loved most.
I tried to be the air you breathed,
But all I was was what you didn't need.
I gave you all that I could give,
But you never saw the way I live.
You took my blood but never knew,
How much I bled just loving you.
My veins run dry, my heart is torn,
You left me cold, alone and worn.
So, I stand here with nothing left to show,
A river of blood, a heart too low.

Letters Never Sent

The Glow That Fades

I'm in love with the man you'll never become,
A shattered dream, a silent hum.
You were a vision I held in my chest,
A fragile form I couldn't arrest.
Like glass that cracks, but never breaks wide,
I'm left to gather what you cast aside.
Twisting and pulling with threads of hope,
Stitching through pain, trying to cope.
I see the glow, your fractured light,
Dimming slowly into endless night.
A flicker lost in a room grown cold,
With the warmth of you, but the heat's turned old.
I curl in your arms and for a breath it's real,
But the warmth dies out and the numbness steals.
The cold creeps back, the hollowness deep,
A cycle of falling I can't help but keep.
You're not what I need, not what I crave,
Just splinters and shards I still try to save.
Needles in hand, I sew through the ache,
But each stitch unravels, each hope I fake.
I wanted the man you never became,
But I'm choosing a ghost, just smoke in the flame.
Trapped in this threadbare, broken design,

Ina Fisher

A love that won't heal, a love out of line.
Each part of you, jagged and torn,
Yet I loved you whole, even when worn.
And though I hold on, I know you won't stay,
For the man I love has drifted away.

Never Loved Out Loud

I got lost beneath the thunder's roar,
No trail to trace, no open door.
Lightning stitches the sky in pain,
Each flash a thread a pulled in vain.
I stretched so thin I turned to glass,
Invisible each time you'd pass.
You never loved me out loud,
Just shadows hiding in a crowd.
Take back your words, they twist like knives,
Your kindness always comes with 'why's'.
"You'll be alright", you softly said,
So, I smiled bright and bled instead.
Then I'll fall in love again,
A cycle steeped in quiet rain.
My heart slipped off my sleeve that day,
No hands to catch it on the way.
You blew the candles out too soon,
Left only ghosts to fill the room.
I'll tell a lie to bring you near,
Even if it costs me tears.
You say you tried but is it true,
Or just another thing you do?
You spun your stories, made them new,
I wasn't enough, well according to you.

Ina Fisher

When the Weather Texts Back

You came in like a hailstorm's kiss,
Sharp and sudden, hard to miss.
The sky turned black, the air stood still,
You touched me once and took your fill.
You message when it suits your night,
A fleeting flame, a borrowed light.
You love me like a one-time drug,
Then vanish cold, no word, no hug.
I think of ways to make you feel,
The ache I carry, sharp and real.
I hope it sinks into your chest,
A bitter echo, no time to rest.
For I'm curating a gallery of pain,
Each face a drop of acid rain.
I rotate them like worn-out songs,
It hurts, but at least it doesn't last as long.
Maybe I'll learn how to walk away,
But I'm the one who begs to stay.
I'm the one who breaks each time,
Still writing love notes in the grime.
The weather's cruel, the winds don't bend,
You never cared, and I pretend.
But even thunder knows what's true,
The storm I hate still sounds like you.

Where Wounds Are

I stare at him like he's a test,
Like every word could be a jest.
What if his warmth is a disguise,
A comfort laced with quiet lies.
He says I'm safe, I want to scream,
Because that phrase has lost its gleam.
So many said the same sweet sound,
Right before they broke me down.
And maybe now I don't believe,
That anyone could really leave
The door unlocked, the edges soft,
And hold me tight without a cost.
My mind replays a thousand scenes,
Where trust was just a war machine.
Where hands once held me then let go,
Where love just meant, you'll never know.
I question him like I'm on fire,
Each kindness met with dust, not desire.
And maybe I'm the haunting one,
The ghost who runs when light has come.
He touches me like I'm not glass,
Like I won't shatter from the past.
He's something I should fear to trust,
But I still learn because I must.

Ina Fisher

Each kindness carves another scar,
Soft hands reminding where wounds are.
And though I tremble in his light,
I stay, half shadow, half in flight.
If love can bloom in fields of pain,
Perhaps I'll learn to love again.

Letters Never Sent

Between Each Relapse

I swore I'd leave, I swore I'd heal,
But broken hearts don't always feel.
I ran to you with open arms,
Forgetting all your quiet harms.
Each time you left, I felt the tear,
Still begging for pieces, you won't spare.
Your silence cuts, your words deceive,
Yet I return, I just can't leave.
You smile like you have done no wrong,
I play along; I sing your song.
But every chorus sounds like pain,
In every verse, a new bloodstain.
I hate you now, or so I claim,
But I still love the sound of your name.
My hate grows sharp, a poisoned kiss,
Yet I still crawl back into this.
It breaks me more, I bend, I snap,
I bleed between each love relapse.
They said, "stay long enough, you'll hate him through",
But they never said it would shatter you too.

Ina Fisher

The Name You Buried

Any love I gave is yours to own,
Like flowers planted in cracked stone.
It bloomed in silence, bruised and deep,
A gift I gave you just to keep.
You carved my name into your trust,
Then left it buried under dust.
I bled from wounds I didn't cause,
Still took the blame without a pause.
So please, make it clean, make it fast,
Say I was just a shadow cast.
A passing phase, a name you crossed,
Not something cherished, only lost.
People like me don't get to stay,
We're borrowed light, then swept away.
We are the anchors others need,
The silent roots from which they feed.
You roam the past with haunted grace,
But find it's just an empty space.
There's no one left, no voice, no flame,
Just echoed walls that know my name.
It hurts to heal with I did not break,
To carry storms I didn't make.
You were the fire, I was the skin,
Burned just for letting you in.

So, lie, if truth feels far too deep,
Say I meant nothing, make me weep.
Because silence stings far worse than hate,
And ghosts like me have learnt to wait.

Ina Fisher

Too Sweet, Too Loud

You were my first, my brightest spark,
A fire that lit up all my dark.
You held me close, then let me go,
And left a pain I'll always know
You came back like a favourite song,
Too sweet, too loud, it feels so wrong.
You whisper love, like you forgot,
The way my heart was left to rot.
You broke me once, without a sound,
I built myself up from the ground.
And now you're here, all soft and sure,
But I remember the before.
You say you've changed, your eyes say 'stay',
But hearts don't heal in just one day.
You love bomb me, then disappear,
And I don't know what's real I fear.
I miss you more than I should dare,
But love like this it isn't fair.
I'm scared to trust, to let you in,
To lose myself to you again.
So don't come close if this won't last,
Don't make me dream about the past.
If you're just here to play pretend,
Then please don't make me break again.

Ink This Pain

I can turn you into poetry,
But I can't make you love me.
Your name still burns in every line,
A ghost I dress in borrowed rhyme.
The sunset bled into the sea,
Like all the dreams you took from me.
Its colours dimmed, then disappeared,
Just like your voice I once held dear.
The sky forgot to hold its hue,
And dusk rolled in, a deeper blue.
A mist crept slow across my chest,
Like sorrows hand that stole my rest.
Hurting me didn't hurt you,
And that's when I knew.
I was the echo, not the sound,
The roots, not flowers above ground.
You left so clean, like morning dew,
That vanishes by half past two.
While I remain, still soaked in ache,
Still writing love you chose to fake.
Fog drifts in where light once lay,
It clouds my heart; it blurs the day.
I reach for shapes that won't stay still,
Like memories bent to your will.

Ina Fisher

A thousand verses cry your name,
But none can set the soul aflame.
You live in metaphors I write,
But never stayed to hold the night.
So, I let the sunset end for good,
No second blaze, no amber wood.
All ink this pain and set it free,
For I can turn you into poetry,
But I can't make you love me.

Poison and Frost

He comes back like winter through a broken pane,
Cold breath, sweet lies, and a hunger for pain.
His voice drips honey, his hands drip frost,
Every return reminds me of what's lost.
I let him in though I'll always bleed,
Craving his poison like it's something I need.
He never stays long, but when he goes,
He leaves me consumed by sorrows.
Tiny splinters beneath my skin,
Whispers buried deep within.
They creep through bone, they crawl through vein,
Each step he takes, a sharper pain.
They move so slow, but they still start,
To inch their way towards my heart.
Not fast enough to scream or fight
Just slow enough to steal my light.
I speak and silence answers back,
My ribs are splinters, white and black.
He doesn't have to raise a hand,
His love alone can reprimand.
With every kiss a deeper sting
A jagged edge on everything.
But glass remembers where it tore,
And I can't be what I was before.

Ina Fisher

I'm not his home, I'm just a place,
He shatters when he needs more space.
And still, I wait. I ache. I burn,
For him to leave or not return.
He knocks. I bleed. I cave. I fall,
And I don't recognise myself at all.

Letting Go In Pieces

It started slow, a blurred hello,
A look that lingered, soft and low.
One night became a line we crossed,
And now I count the things I've lost.
We both agreed it's casual,
But nothing in me felt that dull.
I breathe him in like morning air,
He's in my skin, he's everywhere.
I see him through a dreamer's lens,
The kind reserved for more than friends.
Each little thing, I turn to gold,
A glance, a laugh, a hand I hold.
He says we're chill, just riding time,
But I can't make that lie feel mine.
I live and breathe him I can't do 'just',
When every look feels close to us.
I miss my friend, the one I knew,
Before the space between us grew.
But more than that, I miss the dream,
Of what we were, or what we seemed.
Still maybe just a piece is fine,
To hold love that isn't mine.
But maybe that's enough to keep,
A fragment of him buried deep.

Ina Fisher

Or let it be, I'll let it go,
I live the lie I'm forced to know.
All swallow at this silent ache,
But when I see him, I might break.

Letters Never Sent

Holding Until it Hurts

Everything I've ever let go of has claw marks on it,
My heart wrote its name, but the world painted on it.
I held it close, I held it tight,
But nothing stays yours just because you fight.
The harder I gripped the faster it fled,
Leaving claw marks where love once bled.
Like sand through fingers, quick to fade,
Nothing ever lasts, nothing's ever stayed.
I've let go of love, I've let go of dreams,
Of whispered promises and shattered seams.
The claw marks remain, they won't fade away,
A constant reminder of love gone astray.
I move through the world, I shoulder the weight,
Of everything precious I couldn't save.
Scars on my heart and fire in my soul,
Proof of the things I couldn't control.
I let go but the silence still screams,
Etched in my skin are the ghosts of my dreams.

Ina Fisher

Small Enough to Stay

I need to be small, to shrink and bend,
To swallow my voice and try to pretend.
To stuff down the screams with a sock and a smile,
And live in your hand, for a little while.
To hush every thought that dares to escape,
To mould myself into a likeable shape.
To laugh on command, then quiet again,
So, you might decide I'm worthy, and then
I'll tell myself I'm not witty or wise,
Just a face with a script and agreeable eyes.
The cool girl you wanted, quiet and sweet,
Who walks one step behind your feet.
I'm sorry I spoke, I said far too much,
So, I'll fold myself up, withdraw from your touch.
Tail tucked low, I'll fade from the scene,
And make you the king of this crumbling dream.
I'll swallow the sting, ignore every bruise,
And ask how you are, like I always do.
I'll leave myself waiting, quiet and true,
While making more space, to make room
for you.

Fitting Into Your Rain

I bend beneath your storm skies,
Shape myself to match your lies.
Each drop of rain, a plea I send,
Begging you to want me again.
I fold like paper in your hands,
Moulded by your shifting plans.
A shadow stretched to fill your space,
A hollow mask, a fading face.
The rain falls hard, it beats me down,
But I still crave your empty crown.
I wash away my own design,
To fit the shape, you draw in time.
I'm drowning in this endless rain,
Your silence drips, a slow refrain.
I beg the storm to hold me close,
To want me more than I want most.
But storms don't love, they only take,
And leave behind the hearts they break.
Yet here I stand, still soaked and worn,
Fitting myself into your storm.
No shelter from this love I chase,
No light beyond your cold embrace.
Just endless rain, my hollow plea,
Want me or let me be free.

Ina Fisher

Learning to Live

I carry a heart torn clean in two,
A hollow space where love once grew.
It bleeds in silence, a quiet ache,
A wound that never seems to break.
No bandage here can hold the pain,
No healing balm can ease the stain.
I walk through days with fractured skin,
A map of loss etched deep within.
The edges raw, the scars run deep,
They whisper secrets I can't keep.
I'm learning how to breathe with less,
To find a life inside this mess.
The hollow is both curse and home,
A place where I am left alone,
But in the ache, a truth I find,
That broken hearts can still be kind.
So here I stand, torn, but alive,
With open wounds I still survive.
I'll live with this, my shattered part,
And carry on with my torn-out heart.

www.ingramcontent.com/pod-product-compliance
Lightning Source LLC
Chambersburg PA
CBHW071222070526
44584CB00019B/3117